BONSAI FOR BEGINNERS

The Authoritative GUIDE offer you all you need to know as a beginner

By

Loran James

Copyright@2018

Table of Contents

CHAPTER 1 3
   INTRODUCTION TO BONSAI 3

Chapter 2 11
   The Distinctive Sizes of Bonsai 11

Chapter 3 12
   The requirements for Getting Bonsai 12

Chapter 5 16
   The equipment required. 16

Chapter 6 19
   Cost involve going into Bonsai 19

Chapter 7 22
   Picking Bonsai for your Atmospher condition 22

Chapter 8 33
   The most effective method to Purchase Bonsai Trees 33

CHAPTER 1
INTRODUCTION TO BONSAI

The most effective method to

BONSAI FOR Apprentices: The Authoritative GUIDE offer you all you need to know as a beginner.

Bonsai is a compensating artistic expression and consistently more individuals from all around the globe are beginning to look all starry eyed at it.

In any case, many think that it's difficult to begin... or even make sense of if bonsai is for them.

Prior to the web, getting your hands on bonsai assets was an issue.

Presently the issue is dealing with the large number of assets to make sense of which ones are extraordinary and which ones are not very good.

That is the place this guide comes in.

I've scoured the web and past to locate the best assets for fledglings needing to dunk their toes into the universe of bonsai. This guide won't transform you into a bonsai ace, yet it will enable you to make sense of if bonsai is for you and what your initial couple of steps ought to be.

Chapter by chapter guide

Bonsai can be enormously agreeable, yet it's not for everybody. In this first part we'll take a superior perspective of bonsai and help you make sense of if it's something you need to seek after or whether you're in an ideal situation simply appreciating bonsai from a far distance.

Bonsai More or less

Bonsai has a significant long history returning a thousand years or something like that. While some contend that it was brought over from China, what we consider to be present day bonsai is something that created in Japan in the course of the last couple of hundred years.

Bonsai originates from Japanese where it is comprised of two characters (plate and planting). It is a living fine art that includes taking conventional trees and developing them in pots to confine their development.

The point of a bonsai craftsman is to make falsely consummate trees looking like those in nature. This is inconsistent to the European craft of topiary, where the point is to utilize trees to make something that looks like anything other than a tree.

It is regularly alluded to as a side interest, yet a great many people who are included with bonsai consider it to be a fine art. It is most mainstream in Japan and due to the historical backdrop of the artistic expression there, numerous trees are generational.

In contrast to a depiction or model, a bonsai is never wrapped up. Similarly likewise with a palace, you never really claim a bonsai; you simply deal with it for the people to come.

The Diverse Types of Bonsai

While each bonsai is novel and the craftsman isn't obliged by anything other than his abilities and creative energy, characterization frameworks have developed that can enable specialists to make bonsai that impersonate the type of regular trees.

The five fundamental structures are recorded underneath:

1. Formal upright
2. Informal upright
3. Slanted
4. Semi Cascade
5. Full Cascade

While the above represented the principle five structures, there are bounty more to take a gander at. Since they're past the extent of this guide, in the event that you'd like to find out about the other well-known styles of bonsai, here are some valuable connections:

Bonsai Domain

Bonsai Experience

Wikipedia

Chapter 2
The Distinctive Sizes of Bonsai

Since you decide the extent of the tree with the measure of the pot, when making bonsai, settling on how enormous you need your bonsai to be is another decision you'll need to make.

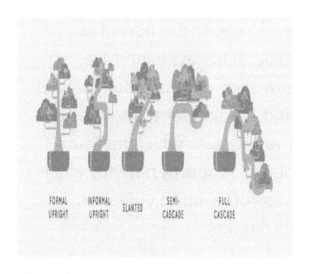

There's no set in stone answer here; you're allowed to chip away at trees that are whatever estimate you like. Right off the bat, think about what size of tree advances to you. This will be distinctive for everybody.

Besides, think about that there are upsides and downsides to each size. Littler bonsai will in general be less expensive, consume up less room (clearly) and are simpler to move and transport, so which measure bonsai is appropriate for you is absolutely up to your own inclination.

In Japan, there are classes of bonsai as per estimate. This is done to some degree to make presentations logical challenge, yet additionally with the goal that the size of a bonsai is comprehended when taking a gander at photographs. Without a reference point it tends to be difficult to measure how huge a specific tree is.

There are a few classes of size, running from the 1-3cm keshitsubo to the two meter tall Majestic Bonsai. Wikipedia has a decent rundown of the distinctive Japanese classes of bonsai. Here's a representation of a portion of the more typical bonsai sizes:

1. Smomin
2. Katede-mochi
3. Chumond
4. Omono
5. Imperial Bonsai

Indoor versus Open air Bonsai

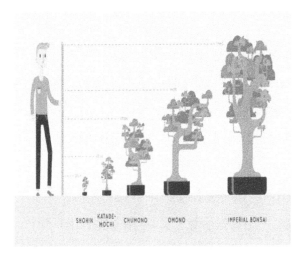

In spite of what many individuals figure, you can't generally develop your bonsai inside. It may entice keep your trees inside with the goal that you can see them while you approach your day, yet the fact of the matter is somewhat more confused.

While a few animal varieties can be developed inside, generally can't. Most trees require a time of lethargy to endure and flourish. In deciduous trees, this period is activated by cool, so in the event that your tree is inside and splashing up your warming, it will never enter this period and it's life expectancy will be constrained.

Getting the perfect measure of light is additionally an issue with indoor bonsai.

Furthermore, in case you're somebody that utilizes cooling, that can likewise be an issue since air on lessens dampness and solid bonsai require some stickiness.

Chapter 3
The requirements for Getting Bonsai

Before beginning with bonsai it's vital to comprehend what you're getting yourself into. Much the same as you wouldn't take responsibility for pet without first understanding the extent of the dedication.

One thing that learners need to know is to what extent it will take before you have your very own wonderful bonsai. When finding out about bonsai it's anything but difficult to run over references to trees that are a hundred years of age.

Obviously not.

To go from a fundamental tree to a bonsai can take a couple of months in case you're cautious and recognize what you're doing. A large portion of the fight is forming your tree, which is represented by the sort of tree and the season.

All things considered, a tree is never "completed"; it's a living being and in this way dependably a work in advancement.

Furthermore, amateurs additionally need to think about how much time is required to style and keep up their bonsai.

It's somewhat similar to dealing with a pet.

It doesn't really require a great deal of investment every day (bonsai don't should be taken for a walk), yet you should put shortly of time every day, and a couple of times each year invest altogether more effort.

Standard watering and preparing doesn't take long, however on the off chance that you neglect to water your bonsai, they won't live long.

Chapter 5
The equipment required.

To fare thee well and style your bonsai you will require some essential hardware.

Julian Adams, an eminent bonsai craftsman, suggests the accompanying bits of gear:

- Sunken pruner

- Bud scissors

- Wire

- Wire cutters

- Handle shaper

- Root snare

- Root shaper

Notwithstanding the abovementioned, you'll likely need a couple of specific odds and ends, for example, a watering can, chopsticks for uncovered establishing, etc.

Adams favors Japanese devices and finds that even shoddy apparatuses from Japan beat progressively costly forms from somewhere else. You can peruse progressively about a portion of the gear required here:

Fundamental Devices for Bonsai by Julian Adams

Another extraordinary article on bonsai devices is by Bonsai Domain.

Chapter 6
Cost involve going into Bonsai

Similarly as with any undertaking, it's useful to know how much a raid into bonsai will set you back.

What's more, similarly as with any undertaking, the genuine number is difficult to bind.

To what extent is a bit of string?

You can obtain your first bonsai for nothing, you can spend a bit, or you can burn through $750,000.

The equivalent applies to gear. You can purchase a modest ten piece set for $50, or burn through $300 on a solitary instrument.

The amount to spend relies upon your dimension of intrigue and your monetary circumstance, yet most would agree that even on a constrained spending you can truly appreciate the specialty of bonsai.

Chapter 7
Picking Bonsai for your Atmosphere condition

One of the components that will restrain what trees you can develop is your atmosphere.

Trees develop best in atmospheres they are indigenous to.

Individuals living in mild atmospheres by and large have an extensive variety of trees to browse, while those from the tropics or sharply cool atmospheres may need to pick their trees with more consideration.

Before you get hold of your first bonsai, verify that the bonsai you need can get by in the atmosphere you live in.

Here are a couple of connections you can use to check what atmosphere zone you're in:

- Australian Atmosphere Zones

- American Plant Strength Zone Guide

- Canadian Temperature Guide

- UK Provincial Atmospheres

- Atmosphere of New Zealand

Most Regular Types of Bonsai

Odds are the point at which you consider bonsai there are a couple of animal groups that fly into your head.

While you can transform any types of tree into bonsai, some have ended up being more prominent than others.

There are many list to get from when you go into further research.

Your First Bonsai

In the event that you have not been frightened away by the data up until this point, making sense of where to get your first bonsai is an intelligent following stage.

What's more, as with everything else bonsai, it's not as direct as you may accept.

Numerous learners begin with a "mallsai", which is a shoddy bonsai generally accessible in shopping centers. These are ordinarily not the most elevated quality trees and keeping in mind that they may be fun, on the off chance that you're not kidding about bonsai, there are different techniques to use to secure your first bonsai.

We will take a gander at the primary five different ways.

One technique is to develop your own bonsai from a seed. There's something unique about taking a shot at a tree that you developed from nothing, however on the off chance that you're in a rush to begin, this isn't the strategy for you since it can take around two years previously the tree is sufficiently able to be styled.

Another strategy is to utilize cuttings. This includes taking branches from a sound tree and after that planting it in soil to develop as another tree. One noteworthy favorable position to this strategy is that the new tree will hold attributes of its parent tree; so if the first was an extremely incredible tree to work with, so will the enhanced one.

Be that as it may, this technique can in any case take a significant long time and on the off chance that you are bonsai-less, finding a tree to get a cutting from can be troublesome.

A third technique is to utilize uniting or layering. Once more, these techniques can require some serious energy and require aptitudes that you likely don't have at this stage. In the event that you'd like to peruse up on layering and uniting, Bonsai

Domain again have some extraordinary articles:

Air Layering as a Bonsai development system

Joining trees as a Bonsai development system

A fourth technique is to discover a tree in the wild that has been obliged commonly. Fanatics of the karate child will recall Mr. Miyagi moving down a precipice face to discover a tree and bonsai discovered along these lines are called yamadori.

Discovering yamadori is fairly a game all by itself in Japan. In any case, this isn't something for the uninitiated to endeavor. In addition to the fact that you need to have the capacity to distinguish which trees are appropriate, however you likewise need to realize how to securely take the tree home.

Also that nowadays there are limitations in many nations regarding what you can lawfully take from woods.

That abandons us with one last technique:

Begin with a bonsai that has effectively developed.

This is most likely the best place to begin since the expectation to learn and adapt is much shallower and it will require you less investment to develop something wonderful.

This strategy isn't without some trouble, be that as it may.

Despite everything you have to figure out how to pass judgment on a tree yourself so you purchase the best tree for your cash. In a perfect world you would have somebody increasingly experienced help with your buy, however in case you're individually.

Chapter 8
The most effective method to Purchase Bonsai Trees

Here's one case of a site that you can purchase trees from:
Nursery Tree Wholesalers

At this stage you ought to comprehend the fundamentals of bonsai and have the capacity to purchase your first tree.

Presently we can move onto section two, where you'll figure

out how to keep that first tree alive!

When you comprehend the fundamentals and have the realize how to get your hands on your first quality tree, you have to figure out how to keep that tree alive and solid.

You can have all the styling abilities on the planet, yet on the off chance that you continue slaughtering trees, those aptitudes will go to squander.

Numerous individuals murder trees when they begin, however on the off chance that you pursue the tips in this part, you won't be one of them!

- **Watering**

Keeping your trees all around watered is one of the essentials of bonsai upkeep.

People can't go long without water and trees aren't vastly different.

On the off chance that you're to wind up a bonsai craftsman, you'll be investing a smidgen of energy watering your accumulation.

And keeping in mind that a great many people comprehend that trees can pass on from absence of water, most are unconscious that overwatering can likewise be deadly to your bonsai.

It shouldn't occur in case you're utilizing great soil, however in the event that an excessive amount of water gets caught inside the pot, the roots can spoil away.

How frequently you have to water, how much water to utilize and what kind of watering can (your customary garden can won't do) are everything you have to consider. Also that the watering timetable will likewise contrast contingent upon the types of tree you use.

The particulars are a little past the extent of this course, however we've discovered a decent guide for you to peruse.

- **The Correct Soil**

Utilizing the correct soil from the get go is likewise critical.

Bonsai soil will in general be ordered by surface and type.

The measure of the pot decides the surface required, yet the sorts of soil is dictated by the types of the tree and whether the tree is being prepared or not.

Picking up a full comprehension of bonsai soil can get dubious rapidly; you have to comprehend the job of soil, seepage factors, and what segments to use (there are numerous to browse).

Here's an incredible guide on Picking Soil for Bonsai, from Kaizen Bonsai.

Furthermore, here's another connect to inquire about done by a part from the Finger Lakes

Bonsai Society that is extremely worth a perused.

- **Repotting Your Bonsai**

Figuring out how to repot your bonsai is another critical aptitude that you'll have to ace in case you're to wind up a bonsai craftsman.

Trees in nature have root frameworks that develop outward looking for supplements.

It's what trees are modified to do.

Your bonsai doesn't have any acquaintance with it's in a pot so its underlying foundations will even now become outward in the worthless endeavor to discover supplements.

At first this isn't an issue, yet in the end the root organize turns out to be so thick and thick that the tree battles to get the supplements it needs.

Before this happens you have to remove your bonsai from its pot, trim the root framework back and after that repot it.

Here's a guide that clarifies the procedure well ordered:

Repotting Bonsai Trees

Indeed, even the best quality soil doesn't keep going forever.

After a specific measure of time, soil separates and is never again ready to carry out its responsibility. Time scales fluctuate, yet five years is about to what extent most soil will last.

At the point when this occurs, you have to supplant the old soil with new soil; this procedure is called exposed establishing.

You'll have to remove the bonsai from its pot and after that cautiously expel the dirt from the roots. Bamboo chopsticks are a well-known device for this specific employment.

Regardless of whether to uncover root your bonsai or not is a challenged theme in the realm of bonsai.

- **Manure**

Trees require supplements to develop and endure simply like individuals, yet bonsai confront a test while getting every one of their supplements.

Trees developing in the wild can search out supplements from wide zones. This is the reason their root frameworks extend far and wide.

Be that as it may, bonsai are obliged by their pot, so they depend on the encompassing soil for their supplements.

This dirt rapidly loses its supplements and consequently so as to keep your bonsai alive you have to supply it with standard compost.

There are a couple of rules to pursue while choosing your compost; the equalization of nitrogen, phosphorus and potassium ought to by and large be kept equivalent.

You should likewise be mindful so as not to overload, since this can harm the roots.

Here's an extraordinary video by Orlando Bonsai television that clarifies bonsai manures in more detail:

Bonsai How to – Composts for Bonsai

- **Bugs**

People aren't the main animals to appreciate bonsai.

Sadly, a few types of bugs can swarm your bonsai and cause it genuine mischief.

Make it a player in your week after week custom to nearly investigate your bonsai for any indications of vermin. Ants, aphids and exhausting bugs would all be able to wreak ruin on your trees, so figure out how to pay special mind to them. Caterpillars and worms are additionally not extraordinary to have around.

Here are a few aides that can help you in distinguishing and treating bugs:

I. Bonsai Bug Security

II. Bonsai Plant Bugs to Look for!

III. Weeding

All together for your bonsai to be as solid and sound as would be prudent, it needs to take in every one of the supplements it needs.

This can't occur if weeds attack your pot and begin taking supplements for themselves, so weeding must be another movement that is a piece of your standard work process.

Weeding is entirely clear, however on the off chance that you'd like somewhat more data on the most proficient method to do it, here's a helpful guide:

The most effective method to weed a Bonsai

Presently you're an ensured green thumb and can keep your

bonsai alive, you can begin to take in the fun stuff.

In this section you'll take in the essentials of styling your bonsai; taking an ordinary tree and changing it into something stunning.

- **Styling Basics**

Styling your bonsai is the fundamental piece of the artistic expression. It's what individuals consider when they consider bonsai and includes truly twisting the tree to your will.

It's not something you do once and after that disregard; styling proceeds for the life of the tree.

Before you do anything extraordinary, ponder the tree in its regular frame. Build up a decent comprehension of what you're meaning to accomplish before you begin the work.

Take a gander at other bonsai for motivation and thoughts of what you could go for.

Many books have been expounded on styling bonsai and we aren't meaning to show you everything here; simply the essentials.

Styling ordinarily starts with the storage compartment.

When the storage compartment is solid, wire the branches into the shape you need. At long last, prune the tree to make it look perfectly.

Clearly doing this is less demanding said than done, so we'll be including a lot of connections at the base of this manual for show you the points of interest of how to style your tree.

Next up we'll investigate what wiring is and how it functions.

- **Wiring Your Bonsai**

You utilize metal wire to twist the tree in the shape you need.

When you twist a tree and keep it there with wire, little parts will show up in the internal layers of the tree. As those parts mend the tree will recall its new position.

To what extent this procedure takes relies upon how rapidly the tree develops. This implies distinctive species will set aside unique measures of opportunity to be prepared.

The season likewise matters.

What's more, which season is best for your tree additionally varies from species to species. Common time spans are from 2-3 weeks to a while relying upon the above factors.

When your bonsai has come to fruition, evacuating the wire accurately is vital so you don't harm the tree. While some accomplished specialists do loosen up it by hand, a lot more essentially cut it off at the curves.

Forming your trees with wire is clearly a central aptitude for styling bonsai, so on the off chance that you'd like to take in somewhat more, here is a phenomenal instructional exercise from Ryan Neil of Bonsai Mirai:

- **Pruning Your Bonsai**

When the storage compartment has been molded and your branches are the place you need them to be, it's a great opportunity to prune the tree.

Once more, this is a confounded subject and not something we're specialists on. So to take in more about pruning your bonsai, you'll need to get your hands on some quality preparing materials.

- **Picking Your Pot**

Bonsai isn't bonsai without a pot, so picking the correct pot for your bonsai is an essential choice.

It's vital for useful reasons, as well as the feel of your pot additionally matters.

The correct pot should show your bonsai to the best favorable position; a similar way a casing does on a work of art.

Normally round pots are best to incline bonsai, while upstanding bonsai look best in oval or rectangular pots.

The shading ought to likewise differentiate the tree. Here are a few recordings that should enable you to pick the correct pot for your bonsai.

The End

Printed in the USA
CPSIA information can be obtained
at www.ICGtesting.com
CBHW071700111224
18829CB00033B/1200